Original title:
Echoes of Wonder

Copyright © 2024 Creative Arts Management OÜ
All rights reserved.

Author: Jaxon Kingsley
ISBN HARDBACK: 978-9916-88-860-5
ISBN PAPERBACK: 978-9916-88-861-2

Reverberations of the Heart

In shadows deep, our whispers play,
Echoes linger, night and day.
A tender pulse, a fluttering sigh,
Hearts entwined as time drifts by.

Through quiet moments, breaths align,
In silent vows, our souls combine.
A melody that knows no end,
The heart's own song, a cherished friend.

Twilight's Veil of Mystery

Underneath the velvet sky,
Stars awaken, spirits fly.
Softly wrapped in twilight's glow,
Secrets hide where shadows grow.

A shimmering dance of light and dark,
Dreams ignite a hidden spark.
In stillness, the night begins to weave,
A tale of magic, believe, conceive.

The Unfolding of Secrets

Pages turn in whispered tones,
Ancient truths in quiet groans.
Each layer peeled, a story rare,
Hidden wonders, light as air.

In the silence, wisdom speaks,
Every riddle, time bespeaks.
Beneath the surface, depths profound,
Lost in echoes, we are found.

A Symphony in the Breeze

Gentle winds weave through the trees,
   Carrying notes of soft decrees.
  Nature's chorus sings so sweet,
   A symphony beneath our feet.

From rustling leaves to echoes clear,
   Every sound draws us near.
  In each breath, the world abounds,
   In harmony, the heart resounds.

Beyond the Gaze of Reality

In shadows deep where whispers dwell,
A world unfolds, a fragile shell.
With dreams as sails, we drift anew,
Beyond the gaze, where wonders grew.

In twilight's arms, the secrets hide,
The stars above, our hearts confide.
With every step through veils of night,
We chase the echoes, seek the light.

Through mist and fog, the journey calls,
With every rise, a soft enthralls.
In realms unknown where spirits play,
Beyond the gaze, we find our way.

A dance of fate, a thread so fine,
In cosmic waves, our souls align.
With every heartbeat, tales unfold,
Beyond the gaze, the world of gold.

The Lattice of Wonder

In gardens where the stories weave,
A lattice formed, the heart believes.
With petals bright and colors bold,
The tales of life, in blooms retold.

Beneath the trees, the laughter flows,
In whispered winds, the secret knows.
Each thread connects, a timeless bond,
The lattice strong, of dreams beyond.

In twilight's glow, the magic stirs,
As night descends, the dreamer purrs.
The woven paths, through time and space,
The lattice of wonder, our embrace.

With every star that lights the way,
In every dusk, in every day,
We find our place, our spirits dance,
In the lattice of wonder, life's romance.

Timeless Echoes

In shadows cast by ancient trees,
Whispers of the past float free.
Memories linger, soft and bright,
Echoes dance in the fading light.

Through winding paths of dreams we tread,
Voices of yesterday, softly said.
The clock ticks slow, yet never dies,
In timeless realms, where silence lies.

The Art of Silence

In stillness, secrets softly dwell,
A world untouched, a quiet spell.
Listen close, let your heart receive,
The deep tales in silence weave.

Breath of wind, the hush of trees,
Nature's song brings gentle ease.
In the pause, wisdom gently flows,
The art of silence, everyone knows.

The Enigma of Days

Morning breaks with golden haze,
Each moment holds a wondrous gaze.
Sands of time slip through the hourglass,
Days unfold as shadows pass.

In twilight's glow, questions arise,
What truths hide beneath the skies?
The enigma wrapped in laughter's play,
We find ourselves, then drift away.

Vibrations of the Soul

In every heartbeat, there's a song,
A rhythm deep where we belong.
Vibrations dance in air so light,
Connecting us, a shared delight.

In laughter's ring and tears of joy,
The soul's embrace, none can destroy.
Through every struggle, every goal,
We find the pulse of the living soul.

The Mirage of Memory

Fleeting whispers in the night,
Shadows dance in soft moonlight.
Fractured dreams long gone astray,
Where sunlit hopes begin to fray.

Chasing glimpses of what was lost,
Each sweet moment, a heavy cost.
Reflections fade in twilight's gleam,
A mirage held within a dream.

Cascades of Inspiration

In twilight's glow, thoughts take flight,
Colors blend into pure delight.
Rivers of ideas flow like streams,
Echoing softly with vibrant dreams.

Mountains echo with ancient lore,
Each creak of time, a mighty roar.
Creativity surges and swells,
As nature's spirit weaves its spells.

Oracles in the Breeze

Whispers traverse the gentle air,
Carried softly, beyond compare.
Leaves rustle secrets of the day,
In quiet tones, they silently say.

Ancient wisdom graces the trees,
Guiding hearts like a cool, sweet breeze.
In every sigh of the passing wind,
A prophecy waiting to be pinned.

The Alchemy of Shadows

In candlelight, shadows weave,
Patterns flicker, hint, and deceive.
Mysteries cloaked in softest night,
Crafting tales from absence of light.

From silence springs a hidden art,
As darkness plays its crucial part.
Transforming doubt into pure insight,
In the alchemy of endless night.

Ripples Through the Veil

Whispers dance upon the tide,
Secrets lost, and dreams abide.
In twilight's gentle, fading light,
The world unfolds, yet hides from sight.

A song of ages, softly sung,
Through veils of time, the past is flung.
With every pulse, the waters sway,
A haunting echo of yesterday.

Shimmers of Untold Stories

Beneath the stars, a tale awaits,
In shadows deep, and open gates.
Each shimmer speaks of paths unseen,
Of lives entwined, a tapestry keen.

The moonlight weaves its silver thread,
In quiet corners where hopes are fed.
A flicker bright, a fleeting glance,
Invites the heart to take a chance.

The Canvas of Existence

Life's brush strokes on a canvas wide,
Colors merge, and worlds collide.
Each moment painted, pure and bold,
A masterpiece beyond the fold.

In every hue, a story flows,
In shadows deep and sunlight's glows.
The canvas stretches, wide and vast,
Embracing futures, honoring past.

Flickers Beneath the Skin

Embers flicker behind closed eyes,
Silent whispers, hidden sighs.
A heartbeat echoes, soft and true,
In stillness, life begins anew.

The pulse of dreams beneath the flesh,
In every touch, emotions mesh.
A dance of souls, a tender spin,
Revealing flickers deep within.

Wanderlust in the Mind's Eye

In the shadows, visions glide,
Across the landscapes of my mind.
Each whisper calls, a world untied,
Infinite journeys yet to find.

Mountains rise beneath the sky,
Oceans beckon with their sighs.
Through valleys deep, and fields wide,
Adventure waits where dreams abide.

Footsteps traced on paths unknown,
Every turn a tale that's grown.
A tapestry of sights and sound,
In this realm, my heart is found.

A compass set among the stars,
Guides the heart, despite the scars.
Wanderlust, a yearning cry,
Forever free, my spirit flies.

Whispers of Infinity

In the quiet, secrets stir,
Echoes dance, as moments blur.
Time unwinds, a soft caress,
Infinite thoughts, I must confess.

Stars entwined in silent grace,
Galaxies spun in endless space.
Each whisper draws me ever near,
To mysteries wrapped in the clear.

Boundless realms of thought unfold,
Tales of warmth and dreams retold.
In shadows deep, the light will gleam,
A universe born from a dream.

Floating on a gentle breeze,
Voices rise among the trees.
Infinity, my heart's embrace,
In every whisper, I find my place.

The Secret Beneath Starlight

Underneath the canopy wide,
Where the velvet dark confides.
Whispers linger, secrets shared,
In the stillness, hearts declared.

Moonbeams cast their silver glow,
Lighting paths where lovers go.
In the dewdrops, dreams alight,
Painting magic through the night.

Ancient tales of love and loss,
Carried by the stars embossed.
In their shimmer, truth can be,
A guide for those who long to see.

With every twinkle, hope ignites,
Binding souls on starry nights.
Underneath this vast expanse,
We find our truth in twilight's dance.

Resonance of Dreams

In the stillness, echoes rise,
Carried on a gentle sigh.
Dreams awaken, softly blend,
In the silence, they transcend.

Whispers of a distant past,
Images in shadows cast.
Every heartbeat bold and true,
Resonates in shades of you.

Through the haze of twilight's grace,
I can feel your warm embrace.
In the tapestry of night,
Dreams and wishes take their flight.

With each moment, we align,
In this dance, your hand in mine.
Resonance in every beam,
In the quiet, we find dream.

Whispers of the Unknown

In the hush of twilight's breath,
Secrets linger, hiding depth.
Voices calling from the night,
Guiding souls with gentle light.

Shadows dance where dreams reside,
Mysteries of the world abide.
Each sigh tells a tale untold,
Whispers weave the threads of old.

Footsteps trace the edges clear,
Every echo, soft yet near.
Lost in thought, we gently roam,
Searching for a place called home.

In silence, feelings intertwine,
Unknown paths through hearts align.
Together, we will find our way,
Embracing night, welcoming day.

Reflections in Starlight

Glimmers dance on waters deep,
Caught in dreams we dare to keep.
Each sparkle tells a story bright,
Reflections cast in purest light.

Beneath the sky where wishes soar,
Chasing hopes from shore to shore.
The moonlight whispers soft and sweet,
Guiding hearts where souls can meet.

Moments linger, time stands still,
In this peace, we find our will.
With every star, a memory glows,
Guiding us where passion flows.

Lost in thoughts that gently sway,
We'll find our truth along the way.
In starlit dreams, we built our fate,
Together, love will not be late.

Chasing Shadows of Curiosity

In twilight's grasp, we start to chase,
Curiosities, a hidden place.
With each step, the shadows blend,
Adventures waiting 'round the bend.

Secrets whispered by the trees,
Carried softly on the breeze.
Questions linger, beckoning light,
Leading us deeper into night.

Eyes wide open, hearts so free,
Wondering what the world could be.
Embracing all that we can find,
Unraveling the threads entwined.

So let us wander, lost yet found,
In mysteries on hallowed ground.
Together, we shall brave the dark,
Igniting dreams, setting spark.

The Enigma of Silent Stars

Silent stars in velvet skies,
Holding truths in endless sighs.
Each twinkle hides a cosmic tale,
A universe where dreams set sail.

Time's embrace in shadows cast,
Moments fleeting, memories vast.
The night unveils what we can't see,
A puzzle formed in mystery.

In their glow, we ask and yearn,
What secrets lie where passions burn?
Guided by the smallest light,
We seek the answers in the night.

As we gaze at heaven's dome,
We find ourselves, we find our home.
In silent stars, we find our place,
A cosmic dance, a sweet embrace.

Phantasmagoria of Life

In shadows dance the vivid dreams,
Whispers soft, like flowing streams.
Colors bleed, and boundaries blur,
In this world, where visions stir.

Time skips lightly, heartbeats race,
Each moment, a fleeting trace.
Through twisted paths, we chase the light,
In phantoms' grasp, we find our flight.

The Rhythm of Enchantment

Stars above, in twinkling gleam,
Nature's voice, a soothing theme.
Leaves that rustle in the breeze,
Carrying secrets through the trees.

Softly hums the night so deep,
While the world is lost in sleep.
Every heartbeat, every sigh,
Plays a tune beneath the sky.

Interludes of Infinity

Between the moments, silence grows,
Infinite paths where time flows.
Thoughts like rivers, wide and free,
Carving valleys of memory.

Echoes linger, whispers play,
In the dance of night and day.
Each breath a step, each glance a sign,
In this realm of the divine.

The Scroll of Secrets

Words inscribed on ancient scrolls,
Guarding tales of timid souls.
Every chapter holds a quest,
Revealing truths that never rest.

In shadows lie the brightest gems,
Thoughts like whispers, hushed diadems.
Unraveling time, we seek to find,
The hidden truths left behind.

Tides of Glimmering Thoughts

Whispers dance on the sea,
Sparkling under the moon's gaze.
Thoughts drift like drifting ships,
Carried forth by gentle waves.

Moments catch in the light,
Fleeting like the tide's song.
Each glimmer a memory,
Surging where dreams belong.

Deep currents of desire,
Bubble beneath the calm.
Rising like soft laughter,
Bringing forth quiet balm.

Tides flow with secrets shared,
Ebbing, flowing, they weave.
In the depths of twilight's glow,
Glimmering thoughts never leave.

Serenades of Unseen Worlds

Silence sings in the twilight,
Notes that brush against the stars.
Each breath a soft melody,
Carried through the cosmic bars.

Faint echoes of laughter rise,
From realms we cannot touch.
Whispers in the dimming light,
Speak of worlds that feel so much.

Unseen paths call to the soul,
Drawing us to distant shores.
Serenades of hidden realms,
Opening celestial doors.

In shadows, beauty unfolds,
Softly like the dawn's embrace.
In the heart of night's silence,
We find our sacred space.

Labyrinths of Delight

Twisting paths of bright visions,
Each turn a new surprise.
In the maze of fleeting joys,
Delight flickers and flies.

Sunbeams trapped in the branches,
Dancing like playful sprites.
Every corner holds a charm,
Wrapped in the soft twilight sights.

Laughter sings through the corridors,
Echoing throughout the air.
Whispers of wonder surround,
Painting dreams everywhere.

In this maze of golden hours,
Time stretches, bends with grace.
Labyrinths of sweet delight,
Embrace us in their space.

Mystical Footprints

On silver sands of the shore,
Footprints tell a tale untold.
Each step a piece of magic,
In the moonlight's gentle hold.

Waves kiss the edges softly,
Wiping traces from the land.
Yet memories linger brightly,
In the tides of time's great hand.

Every stride leaves a whisper,
Of journeys long and wide.
Mystical paths lay before us,
In the ebbing, flowing tide.

As stars blink above our heads,
Guiding us with hidden light,
Footprints lead to realms unknown,
Where dreams dance through the night.

Journeys through the Unknown

Across the horizon, shadows play,
Footsteps echo where dreams stray.
Each path whispers a hidden tale,
In the silence, courage prevails.

Stars guide the soul through night's embrace,
With every breath, we seek our place.
Mountains rise and rivers flow,
In the unknown, we learn to grow.

Waves crash on shores of time unwound,
Adventure calls from deep profound.
With open hearts, we roam the wild,
In every journey, remain a child.

The compass spins, the map untold,
In swirling mists, the brave and bold.
We chart the skies, embrace the swell,
In journeys vast, we cast our spell.

The Tapestry of Time

Threads of moments woven tight,
In colors bold and shades of light.
Past and present dance as one,
In the fabric, life has spun.

Embroidered dreams in every seam,
Echoes trace the heart's true beam.
Frayed edges tell of battles fought,
In every stitch, a lesson taught.

Ripples of laughter, tears unfurl,
In the weave, we find our swirl.
Golden hours, silver pains,
Together form the soul's refrains.

History whispers in the thread,
Stories of love and hope widespread.
A tapestry rich with every hue,
In every heart, a journey new.

Illuminated Secrets

In shadows deep, the whispers glow,
Secrets held in silken flow.
Flickering candles cast their light,
On the paths that blend with night.

Beneath the surface, truths reside,
In the silence, fears abide.
With every heartbeat, a story starts,
Illuminated by open hearts.

Veils of mystery softly part,
Revealing whispers to the heart.
In shadows where the soft winds blow,
Lies a world few ever know.

Dancing flames conjure the past,
A fleeting glimpse that cannot last.
In twilight's arms, the secrets gleam,
Awakening the quiet dream.

Chords of Enigmatic Beauty

In whispers soft, melodies play,
Enchanting tunes that drift away.
Strings of silence, hearts entwine,
In chords of beauty, deep and fine.

Nature sings in every breeze,
A symphony that aims to please.
Notes like petals falling free,
In harmony, the soul finds glee.

Time stands still in vibrant sound,
In echoes deep, our dreams are found.
Resonating through the night,
Chords of wonder, pure delight.

An orchestra of stars above,
Playing the tunes of hope and love.
In every heartbeat, the music flows,
Through enigmatic beauty, life bestows.

Fantasies in Fragments

Scattered dreams on whispered winds,
Echoes of laughter, where joy begins.
Colors that dance in the twilight glow,
Moments like petals, gently they flow.

Fragments of stories woven in time,
Each one a heartbeat, a cherished rhyme.
Lost in the echoes, we search for the light,
Fantasies linger, elusive and bright.

Reflections in the Mist

Silent shadows in morning's embrace,
Whispers of dreams in a hazy space.
Footsteps align with the shroud of the dawn,
Mirrored in stillness, we ponder and yawn.

Ripples of thought in the fog unconfined,
Secrets that linger, in silence entwined.
Figures emerge, then they vanish from view,
Reflections of life, we're lost in the hue.

Whirlwinds of Imagination

Spinning thoughts like leaves in a gale,
Chasing the moments where dreams prevail.
Ideas collide in a vibrant display,
Whirlwinds of wonder, they twist and sway.

Fleeting visions, like smoke in the air,
Crystals of concept, sparkling and rare.
In the tempest of thought, we freely explore,
Whirlwinds of imagination forevermore.

Paradoxes of Light

Shadows and brilliance in dance they partake,
Each hue a question, a choice we must make.
Flickers of hope in the darkest of night,
Paradoxes woven in strands of pure light.

Mirrors reflect what our eyes cannot see,
Truths intertwined in the fabric of free.
In every glimmer, a story unfolds,
Paradoxes of light, their beauty untold.

The Language of Dreams

In the silence of night, they call,
Whispers float softly, like a ball.
Visions woven, threads of light,
Carrying secrets through the night.

Eyes closed tight, we drift away,
Into realms where shadows play.
Stories told in muted hues,
Where the heart learns to choose.

Shapes of hope and fears collide,
Where the unseen worlds abide.
Through the silence, thoughts take flight,
In the language of dreams, we write.

Like the morning dew on grass,
These fleeting moments slowly pass.
But in our souls, they leave a trace,
The language of dreams, a sacred space.

Elysian Whispers

Beneath the willow's gentle sway,
Elysian whispers softly play.
Embers dance on evening's breath,
Through the dusk, we feel no death.

Petals drifting in twilight's light,
Echoes of the day's delight.
Where wishes glide on silken streams,
Spun from the fabric of our dreams.

Stars awaken in velvet skies,
Painting stories, ancient ties.
With every sigh, the heart's embrace,
As Elysian whispers fill the space.

Moments captured, fleeting, sweet,
In quietude, our souls meet.
A dance of shadows, light, and air,
Elysian whispers everywhere.

Flickering Starlight

Flickering starlight, guides our way,
Through the veil where dreams do play.
Every twinkle, a silent song,
Calling us where we belong.

In the depth of the cosmic sea,
Whispers of time call to thee.
Moments fold in harmony,
Starlight's grace, our symphony.

Across the canvas, shadows dance,
Hope ignites with every chance.
Radiance of the night's embrace,
Flickering starlight, a warm trace.

In the hush, the magic gleams,
Guiding the heart towards its dreams.
With every pulse, the universe sighs,
Flickering starlight in our eyes.

The Palette of the Sky

The palette of the sky unfolds,
In hues of pink and burning golds.
Brushstrokes dance on azure seas,
As the sun bids day to seize.

Clouds become the artist's hand,
Creating scenes so grand and planned.
Each sunset speaks of tales untold,
In colors vibrant, brave, and bold.

Night then blankets the world with care,
Stars like jewels, a precious pair.
In the quiet, twilight sighs,
The palette of the sky never lies.

Dreamers gaze and hearts ignite,
In the colors of the night.
The sky a canvas, ever free,
A timeless dance for you and me.

Harmony of Forgotten Tales

In shadows deep where whispers dwell,
Old stories dance, they weave a spell.
Their echoes rise, soft and sweet,
In quiet corners, memories meet.

Through time they flow like rivers wide,
In hearts of those who dream and bide.
Each tale a thread in life's great loom,
We find our light, dispelling gloom.

From ancient woods to starry skies,
The voices call, as time complies.
In every heart, their song resides,
A tapestry where hope abides.

Let us remember, let us share,
The whispers sweet, beyond compare.
With every tale, a bridge we build,
With open hearts, let love be spilled.

The Soliloquy of Nature

In rustling leaves, the secrets sigh,
The mountains stand, against the sky.
A river's song, a bird's soft song,
Nature's voice where we belong.

The whispering winds, they carry dreams,
Through sunlit fields and silver streams.
A tranquil sigh from trees so tall,
In nature's arms, we feel it all.

Beneath the stars, the world awakes,
With every dawn, a new heart breaks.
The earth extends a gentle hand,
In harmony, our spirits stand.

So pause awhile, and listen near,
To nature's song, both bright and clear.
In every breath, a tale unfolds,
A timeless truth that nature holds.

Chasing Fleeting Moments

Time slips through like grains of sand,
Moments lost, like echoes spanned.
In laughter bright and tears that fall,
We chase the fleeting, hear the call.

A fleeting glance, a whispered breeze,
In fleeting dreams, the heart finds ease.
Each second counts, so hold it tight,
For in its grasp, we find our light.

Though shadows stretch as day turns night,
In fading hues, we find our flight.
Those moments shared will never fade,
In memories sweet, our love is laid.

So dance through time, embrace the thrill,
In every heartbeat, find the will.
To chase the seconds, make them ours,
In fleeting moments lies the stars.

Unraveled Mysteries

In whispered dark, the secrets sleep,
The heart of night, where shadows creep.
With every turn, a clue unfolds,
In hidden paths, the story molds.

From ancient scripts to stars above,
In every truth, we seek for love.
The puzzles weave through time and space,
In every heart, the quest we trace.

The echoes call, a siren's song,
Through tangled threads where we belong.
With courage bright, we pierce the veil,
Unraveling doubts, we set our sail.

So let us seek the light within,
In every loss, there's still a win.
Unraveled fates are ours to claim,
In every mystery, find our name.

When Silence Speaks

In quiet corners shadows lie,
Whispers dance where echoes sigh.
A heart listens, a mind believes,
In every pause, a truth retrieves.

Words unspoken, heavy air,
Emotions weave in silent prayer.
In the stillness, secrets flow,
The soul knows what it cannot show.

Moments stretch with gentle grace,
In silence, we find our true face.
Unraveled thoughts in darkness creep,
In the soft hush, the heart will leap.

Listen close, the world will tell,
In the silence, it's easy to dwell.
For every silence, there's a sound,
When silence speaks, the lost are found.

Underneath the Surface of Time

Hidden layers, deep and wide,
Where memories and dreams abide.
Each tick a story, each tock a thread,
Weaving tales of the lives we've led.

A river flows beneath the skin,
Time's embrace, both loss and win.
Moments linger, shadows cast,
In the depth, the future meets the past.

Hours flutter, ghosts in flight,
Chasing whispers, fading light.
Beneath the clock, a heartbeat strong,
A tapestry where we all belong.

In the silence, echoes chime,
Revealing truths, so sublime.
Beneath each second, life unfolds,
In every breath, the universe holds.

Anthems of the Unsung

In quiet corners, heroes rise,
With humble hearts and tearful eyes.
Their stories woven, threads unseen,
An anthem sung where they have been.

Fingers calloused, dreams pursued,
In the shadows, strength imbued.
Unsung battles, silent cries,
In every struggle, hope defies.

Recognition lost in daily grind,
Yet in their hearts, the dreams align.
They march forward, spirits free,
Believing in what they can be.

So here's to those who fade from view,
In every heart, their courage grew.
Anthems played without a sound,
In whispered dreams, their truth is found.

The Gaze of Infinite Eyes

Above the world, stars watch and wait,
Infinite eyes, a cosmic fate.
They blink in rhythm, a timeless dance,
In their gaze, we find our chance.

Each twinkle tells a tale untold,
Of love and loss, the brave and bold.
In silence, they witness our plight,
Guiding us through the darkest night.

We look up, seeking to know,
What mysteries in starlight glow.
In every shadow, light appears,
The gaze of stars calms our fears.

So lift your eyes and let them see,
The dreams we hold, the souls we plea.
For in the heavens, we are not alone,
The gaze of infinite eyes calls us home.

Languages of the Universe

Whispers of stars in night's embrace,
Galaxies dance in silent grace.
Each planet speaks a tale untold,
In cosmic dreams, mysteries unfold.

Asteroids sing of ancient days,
While comets weave through celestial ways.
Nebulas cradle the light of hope,
As the universe spins in a grand scope.

Lightyears connect hearts so far,
Each glance a bridge, each wish a star.
In the void, our voices blend,
In the silence, our souls transcend.

Horizons of Forgotten Lore

In the mist where shadows play,
Ancient tales begin to sway.
Echoes linger in twilight's gleam,
Whispers of an age, a lost dream.

Mountains stand as wise old men,
Guardians of secrets lost to men.
Rivers flow with laughter, tears,
Tales of joy and hidden fears.

In the crumbling ruins, we find,
Stories etched in every mind.
Horizons hold a timeless quest,
In forgotten lore, we are blessed.

The Fabric of Wonderment

Threads of light and shadow weave,
In the tapestry, we believe.
Every color tells a story,
In the fabric, hidden glory.

Moments stitched in time and space,
Emotions dance, a soft embrace.
Laughter sewn with whispered sighs,
In our hearts, the magic lies.

Wonders twirl in dreams we share,
Every heartbeat, every prayer.
Through the layers, we explore,
In wonderment, we seek for more.

A Symphony of Hidden Realms

In the silence, music brews,
Undiscovered paths, hidden views.
A symphony of stars and dreams,
Each note a mystery that redeems.

Nature sings a timeless tune,
Underneath the silver moon.
Voices rise in harmony,
Revealing realms of fantasy.

Every rustle, every sigh,
Invites us to question why.
In the echoes, secrets glide,
A symphony where dreams reside.

Wonders in the Echo

In the forest where secrets lie,
Soft whispers call from on high.
Each rustle tells a hidden tale,
Of journeys lost, in the veil.

A brook babbles with gentle grace,
Mirroring the stars' embrace.
Every echo, a fleeting sound,
In nature's arms, forever found.

Mossy stones and ancient trees,
Dance with shadows in the breeze.
The world enchants, a mystic show,
Each moment ripe, where wonders grow.

In silence profound, hearts awake,
To unseen bonds that we create.
With each step, in this sacred land,
We write our story, hand in hand.

The Light in Twilight

As daylight fades into the night,
Colors blend, a wondrous sight.
Stars peek out with a shy embrace,
Inviting dreams in their gentle space.

Dusk wraps all in soft-spun gold,
Whispers of stories yet untold.
The horizon glows, a fiery line,
Where shadows dance, and hopes entwine.

Crickets sing, the world grows calm,
Nature's breath, a soothing psalm.
In twilight's arms, we find our way,
Guided by the end of day.

Each moment shared, a cherished thread,
As night descends, our fears are shed.
In the tranquil glow, love ignites,
Together we bask in the coming nights.

Serendipitous Discoveries

Amidst the clutter, treasures hide,
Glimmers of joy when we decide.
A chance encounter, a secret lane,
New paths to walk, no longer plain.

Forgotten books with pages worn,
Old photographs, memories reborn.
A melody played on a distant street,
In every moment, life is sweet.

A gentle smile from a stranger's face,
In serendipity, we find our place.
Every twist, a story unfolds,
Like the warmth of the sun, in the cold.

In laughter shared or silence known,
We weave our stories, seeds are sown.
With open hearts, the world we roam,
In pleasant surprises, we find our home.

The Glimpse of Infinity

On a quiet eve beneath the stars,
We ponder life, neath moonlit scars.
A single breath, a fleeting thought,
In this moment, all we sought.

The universe, a canvas wide,
Galaxies swirl like a cosmic tide.
Each heartbeat echoes the endless span,
In our spirits, the cosmos' plan.

As time stands still, we start to see,
The threads of fate, intertwining free.
In every glance, a boundless space,
Infinite thoughts, in time and place.

So let us dream, with eyes unsealed,
Embrace the wonders, the truth revealed.
For in our hearts, we hold the key,
To glimpse the vastness of eternity.

Constellations of Belief

In twilight's glow, dreams take flight,
Stars whisper secrets, wrapped in night.
Each twinkle spins a tale profound,
A universe of hope, where love is found.

Across the vast and endless shore,
Faith ignites, forevermore.
In every shadow, light persists,
Guiding souls through fate's twists.

Galaxies dance in silent grace,
Each heartbeat echoes in this space.
With every wish upon the high,
Constellations shine, they never lie.

Bound by dreams, we reach and strive,
In belief's embrace, we come alive.
Together we wander the cosmic sea,
Finding strength in unity.

A Whisper Beyond Time

In quiet moments, whispers weave,
Tales of love that never leave.
Through ages past, they softly beckon,
In every heart, their echoes reckon.

Time stands still in this gentle hush,
Memories linger, in every rush.
Softly spoken, a truth divine,
Carried across the sands of time.

Each breath taken, a bond it binds,
In shadows cast, our spirit finds.
A thread of light that softly glows,
Connecting souls in love's sweet throes.

Beyond the years, beyond the pain,
In whispered tones, our hopes remain.
A tapestry of dreams we share,
Suspended in the timeless air.

The Heart's Canvas

Upon the canvas, colors blend,
Strokes of passion, love transcend.
A vibrant hue of joy and pain,
In every corner, truth and chain.

With brushes dipped in dreams anew,
We paint our lives in shades of blue.
Each layer adds a story bold,
In the heart's gallery, treasures unfold.

Textures soft, and edges rough,
Life's outline traced, both sweet and tough.
In shades of crimson, courage glows,
A masterpiece that ever grows.

Together we'll create the art,
Of fleeting moments, heart to heart.
In every color, we find our place,
The heart's canvas, a sacred space.

The Palette of the Heart

A palette rich, of vibrant shades,
Each color tells of dreams we made.
From gentle pastels, soft and light,
To bold and vivid, igniting night.

With every stroke, our stories bloom,
In hues of hope, dispelling gloom.
Together we blend, our spirits rise,
Creating beauty beneath the skies.

The gold of laughter, the green of peace,
In this creation, hearts find release.
With every mixture, we redefine,
A masterpiece that feels divine.

In unity, we craft our fate,
In the palette of love, we celebrate.
Every heartbeat, a song apart,
Painting forever, the palette of the heart.

Harmonies in the Quiet

In the stillness of the night,
Whispers weave through the air,
Stars hum their gentle song,
Peaceful hearts find solace there.

Moonlight paints the world bright,
Casting shadows soft and mild,
Nature's voice, a sweet delight,
In the calm, the spirit smiled.

Crickets chirp in soft refrain,
Leaves rustle in gentle sighs,
Echoes dance in sweet disdain,
Underneath the vast, open skies.

Moments linger, soft and pure,
Time stands still, a sacred grace,
In the quiet, we endure,
Finding beauty in the space.

Fragments of Celestial Journeys

Comets trace their fiery paths,
Constellations share their tales,
Galaxies in endless dance,
Whispers woven in the trails.

Nebulas bloom amidst the dark,
Colors sing in vibrant hues,
Planets spin with timeless spark,
Travelers lost, but never lose.

Lightyears echo dreams untold,
Wonders crafted in the night,
Stars align, both brave and bold,
In the vastness, hearts take flight.

Celestial bodies, shifting grace,
Eternal dance, a cosmic play,
Fragments find their rightful place,
In the universe, we sway.

The Allure of Hidden Paths

Whispers call from trails unknown,
Underneath the ancient trees,
Footsteps linger, seeds are sown,
In the breeze, a gentle tease.

Rivers winding through the green,
Secrets lost in nature's maze,
Every turn, a sight unseen,
In the shadows, beauty plays.

Mossy stones beneath our feet,
Echoes of the past remain,
Paths where time and silence meet,
In their embrace, we feel no pain.

Every journey, fresh and new,
Every choice, a chance to find,
On these hidden paths, we grew,
Discovering the ties that bind.

Dances of Light and Shadow

Sunset casts its golden glow,
Daylight bows to twilight's grace,
Silhouettes put on a show,
In the fading light, they trace.

Moonbeams twirl on silver streams,
Stars join in the cosmic waltz,
Whispered secrets blend with dreams,
In this realm, no room for faults.

Shadows play upon the ground,
Shapes that shift with every sigh,
In their movement, joy is found,
Underneath the endless sky.

Light and shadow dance as one,
Harmony in every beat,
Day and night, they come undone,
In their fusion, life's complete.

Lullabies of the Universe

Stars whisper softly in the night,
Calling dreams to take their flight.
Moonlight dances on the sea,
Singing lullabies, wild and free.

Galaxies swirl in cosmic tune,
Cradling hearts beneath the moon.
Waves of silence, gentle breath,
Embrace the dark, escape found death.

Dreams take shape in shades of light,
Floating softly, taking flight.
In the hush of evening's grace,
The universe holds a warm embrace.

Close your eyes, let worries cease,
In the starry night find peace.
Listen closely, hear the sighs,
The universe sings lullabies.

Trails of the Imagination

Footprints left on sandy shores,
Imagination opens doors.
Winding paths through forest deep,
Where secrets hide and dreamers leap.

Colors splash upon the skies,
Painting visions with their cries.
In the meadow, whispers call,
With every breeze, let shadows fall.

Time stands still on mountain peaks,
Where every heart believes and seeks.
Through the valleys of our mind,
Endless journeys we shall find.

Follow trails that twist and bend,
In dreams where wonders never end.
Let your spirit soar and fly,
In the realms where dreams don't die.

The Breath of Ancient Wonders

Echoes of time dance on the breeze,
Whispers of ancients stir the trees.
In shadows long of towering stone,
Secrets of ages, we have known.

Rivers flow through valleys wide,
Carving stories, deep and tried.
Mountains rise with tales to tell,
Of battles fought and love's sweet spell.

In every leaf, a history lives,
Ancient echoes, the Earth forgives.
Footsteps mark where wisdom dwells,
In the silence, knowledge swells.

Breathe in deep, the ancient air,
Feel the magic resting there.
With every moment, forge ahead,
Embrace the past, let it be tread.

Threads of Enchantment

In twilight hours, the magic spins,
Weaving tales where wonder begins.
Threads of silver, gold, and light,
Stitching dreams through day and night.

Whispers linger upon the thread,
Following paths where hopes are led.
Every knot a story shared,
In the fabric, hearts ensnared.

Enchanted colors blend and swirl,
Creating a tapestry that twirls.
Each hue a feeling, deep and bright,
Threads of enchantment, pure delight.

Gathered close, let imaginations roam,
For in these threads, we find our home.
Woven closely, never apart,
In every stitch, we share our heart.

Murmurs in the Twilight

Whispers drift with the fading light,
Soft secrets wrapped in the night.
Stars blink gently, a tranquil sigh,
Casting echoes across the sky.

The trees sway to an unseen tune,
Shadows dance beneath the moon.
Crickets sing their serenade,
In twilight's calm, where dreams are laid.

A breeze brushes against the skin,
Inviting thoughts to roam within.
Each sigh of dusk a gentle kiss,
In these moments, we find bliss.

As night unfolds its velvet cloak,
The heart speaks softly, words unbroke.
Murmurs linger, sweet and clear,
In twilight's arms, we draw near.

Reverberations of the Heart

Echoes of love in every stare,
Resonating truth we both share.
Notes of passion softly blend,
In this music, we transcend.

The rhythm beats in perfect time,
Carried forth like whispered rhyme.
Every heartbeat, vibrant and bold,
Tales of our journey yet untold.

In silence, a language so deep,
Woven dreams that we both keep.
With every glance, the chorus swells,
Reverberations, like distant bells.

Together we dance, two souls entwined,
In the melody that fate designed.
Through the echoes, love will flow,
In every moment, let it grow.

Shadows of Enchantment

In the gloam where secrets play,
Shadows twist at the end of day.
Mysteries hidden in twilight's grace,
Enticing whispers in soft embrace.

Glimmers of magic paint the night,
As stars twinkle with pure delight.
Underneath the boughs so wide,
Fate and dreams collide and glide.

The moon casts spells of silver hue,
Enchantments pulling me to you.
Like fleeting moments, lost in time,
In this realm, our hearts can rhyme.

With every step, the shadows sway,
Guiding us through the haunting ray.
In this dance of the unknown,
We find a world we can call home.

Lullabies of the Cosmos

Stars hum softly to the night,
Lullabies of purest light.
Galaxies swirl, a gentle play,
Singing softly, come what may.

Comets streak with cosmic grace,
Drawing wishes in their trace.
Nebulae in colors rare,
A soothing balm, a tender care.

The universe cradles time and space,
In its embrace, a warm embrace.
Each heartbeat reverberates wide,
In this vastness, we confide.

Let the cosmos rock us to sleep,
While celestial dreams we keep.
With every sigh, the stars align,
In lullabies, your hand in mine.

The Scribe of Dreams

In twilight's glow, a tale unfolds,
A scribe in shadows, secrets hold.
With quill in hand, he writes the night,
Filling the world with whispered light.

Each dream, a page, a life begun,
In realms of thought, where hopes do run.
His ink, a stream of endless thought,
In every drop, a dream is caught.

He dances through the starlit skies,
Collecting wishes, truth, and lies.
With every stroke, the magic flows,
In spirals wild, where longing grows.

The dawn arrives, the shadows wane,
Yet still his heart holds fast the stain.
For dreams are threads we weave and bend,
In stories shared, we find our end.

Threads of Imagination

In threads of gold, the dreams are spun,
A tapestry of all we've done.
Each color bright, a thought alive,
In every stitch, our hopes revibe.

A loom of stars, a cosmic dance,
We weave our fate, we take the chance.
With every strand, a story told,
In gentle hues, both bold and cold.

Through valleys deep and mountains high,
Our threads entwine, like birds on high.
Imagination, a timeless thread,
In vibrant whispers, we are led.

As dawn breaks through with softest light,
The woven dreams take lofty flight.
In every heart, a spark ignites,
Threads of imagination, endless heights.

The Veil of Enchantment

A whisper floats, the night is near,
The veil of magic draws us here.
In silver mist, the secrets play,
Where wishes bloom and shadows sway.

Beneath the stars, the fairies dance,
In hidden glades, a fleeting glance.
With laughter sweet and voices clear,
They weave the night, dispel our fear.

Enchantments linger, soft and bright,
In every heartbeat, pure delight.
A world awash in dreams and care,
Shrouded in whispers, light as air.

As dawn approaches, magic fades,
But in our hearts, the glow cascades.
The veil remains, though sight is lost,
In dreams we linger, love's sweet cost.

The Pulse of Existence

In every beat, a story spun,
The pulse of life, a race begun.
In every breath, a chance to feel,
A moment's joy, a wound to heal.

The rhythm flows, through hearts it goes,
A river deep, where passion flows.
From dawn's embrace to twilight's sigh,
We dance in time, both low and high.

Through trials faced, our spirits grow,
In silent storms, the courage shows.
Each heartbeat strong, a force to trust,
A pulse of dreams, in hope we thrust.

So feel the beat, let shadows part,
Embrace the pulse that stirs your heart.
For in this life, we find our place,
In every rhythm, love's warm grace.

Secrets Beneath the Surface

Whispers echo in the deep,
Where shadows dance and secrets keep.
Hidden truths in the dark dwell,
Stories woven, none can tell.

A ripple stirs, the surface breaks,
Silent mysteries the water takes.
Glimmers of light, a fleeting glance,
Inviting hearts to take a chance.

Beneath the waves, a world unknown,
In tranquil depths, the past has grown.
A treasure chest of ancient lore,
Waiting patiently on the ocean floor.

Secrets whisper from below,
In tides that ebb, in currents' flow.
The heart shall seek, the mind shall yearn,
For the hidden tales that tides discern.

The Horizon's Muse

Golden rays kiss the day's edge,
Colors blend like a soft pledge.
A palette rich, a canvas wide,
Where dreams and twilight gently bide.

Waves of cerulean stretch and sway,
To the horizon, the heart's ballet.
Clouds painted in hues of desire,
Each sunset ignites a new fire.

In silence, the world holds its breath,
As daylight bows, embracing death.
Yet in that fade, a promise gleams,
For every close births new dreams.

The horizon calls, a siren's plea,
To those who wander, longing to see.
A journey begins as the sun dips low,
In twilight's grace, the moments flow.

Mosaic of Reflections

Fragments scatter, a brilliant spark,
In life's mirror, we leave our mark.
Each piece tells a tale unique,
In colors bold, in whispers meek.

Cascades of memories intertwine,
Bound by echoes, life's design.
Shattered dreams gleam like fine glass,
A tapestry woven as moments pass.

With every shard, a story unfurls,
Layers entwined in a dance of worlds.
In the mosaic, we find our place,
Reflections shimmer, a warm embrace.

From the chaos, beauty does rise,
In the silence, the heart defies.
A symphony crafted from what we've known,
In every glimpse, a love has grown.

Celestial Canvases

Stars adorn the velvet night,
Painted dreams in silver light.
Galaxies swirl in cosmic art,
A canvas vast, where wonders start.

Planets dance in silent grace,
In the vastness, we find our place.
Moons cast shadows, soft and bright,
Guiding hearts through the endless night.

Comets streak like wishes flown,
In the darkness, seeds are sown.
A universe hums a timeless tune,
In every star, a secret moon.

Celestial brushes stroke the skies,
Painting stories, where mystery lies.
In the vast expanse of the night's embrace,
We discover ourselves in the starlit space.

Phantoms of Curiosity

Whispers echo in the dark,
Secrets hiding, leaving a mark.
Eyes wide open, hearts aflame,
Seeking answers, playing the game.

Shadows flicker, questions rise,
In the depths, a yearning cries.
The unknown calls, a siren's song,
In this journey, we all belong.

Mysteries twirl in the night,
Dancing softly, dimming light.
Chasing phantoms, we wander near,
Curiosity fueling each fear.

Through the maze of thoughts we stray,
Dreaming dreams that drift away.
But in the chase, we're truly free,
In phantoms, we find our key.

The Dance of Time

Ticking clocks, a rhythmic sound,
Moments lost, yet profoundly found.
In the spiral, we twirl and sway,
Each heartbeat marks a fading day.

Past and future, intertwined,
In this waltz, we are resigned.
Each step forward, a glance behind,
In time's embrace, our fate is signed.

Seasons change, like flowing streams,
In this dance, we weave our dreams.
Memories twinkle, stars above,
Time spins softly, wrapped in love.

As the curtain falls at last,
We hold the echoes of the past.
In every move, a story told,
In the dance of time, we find our gold.

Beyond the Veil of Reality

Curtains drawn on a silent stage,
Reality bends, frees the cage.
Beyond the veil, whispers glide,
Where dreams and truths gently collide.

Illusions shimmer in the light,
Threads of fate woven tight.
Visions flicker, shadows play,
In the realm where worlds sway.

Secrets hidden, softly sigh,
In the depths, the spirits fly.
Through the doorway, mystery calls,
Beyond the veil, the curtain falls.

In this journey, we will find,
Truths and visions intertwined.
Unlocking wonders, fears laid bare,
Beyond the veil, we learn to care.

Fables in the Wind

Tales spun softly, like gentle breeze,
Fables carried through rustling trees.
Stars listen close to stories old,
In the nighttime, secrets unfold.

Whispers dance on the edge of night,
Woven through shadows, taking flight.
Heroes brave and legends grand,
In every story, unity stands.

Dreams of glory, courage bright,
In the dawn, they chase the light.
As the tales embrace the skies,
Fables in the wind never die.

Here we gather, hearts entwined,
Each whispered tale, a thread defined.
In the wind, truths find their voice,
Fables shared, we all rejoice.

Silhouettes of Reverie

In twilight's grasp, shadows dance,
Whispers flow, a fleeting chance.
Dreams unfold like twilight's thread,
Carried softly, where hearts are led.

Moonlit paths and silent sighs,
Lost in wonder, where time flies.
Echoes linger in the night,
Guiding souls with gentle light.

Fleeting moments, a soft embrace,
Captured in a timeless space.
Through the haze, we seek to find,
The essence of a wandering mind.

In the silence, visions bloom,
Crafted from a starlit loom.
Silhouettes in dreams unfurl,
Painting hope in a shadowed whirl.

The Gallery of Possibilities

In every corner, stories lie,
Waiting for a curious eye.
Canvas blank, a world anew,
Awaiting strokes of bold debut.

Colors clash, then harmonize,
Dreams unfold beneath the skies.
Frames of hope and realms unknown,
A universe of seeds is sown.

Time's brush sweeps across the hues,
Each moment whispers, 'Choose, choose!'
From chaos springs a perfect view,
The gallery beckons, bold and true.

With every path, a tale unfolds,
Stories rich, and visions bold.
Step inside this vibrant space,
Embrace the beauty, life's embrace.

Petals of Perception

Falling softly, petals drift,
Carried gently, nature's gift.
Colors fade in tender hue,
Whispering secrets, old and new.

In the garden, thoughts entwine,
Life's reflections, clear, divine.
Each soft shade, a tale to share,
Echoes linger in the air.

Through the lens, we see it all,
Nature's wonders, great and small.
Petals dance on breezes light,
A canvas formed in morning's bright.

From the ground where dreams take flight,
Perceptions bloom in day and night.
In this symphony of grace,
Life unfolds in every space.

Portraits of the Hidden

In shadows deep, the stories hide,
Layers waiting, side by side.
Whispers caught in silent frames,
Every heart a place of names.

Brushes trace the lines of fate,
Capturing moments, small and great.
Color spills, emotions blend,
A tapestry we dare to send.

Through the lens, we find the soul,
Stories linger, making whole.
Hidden truths in light revealed,
In a portrait, hearts congealed.

Every gaze a tale retold,
In brush and canvas, dreams unfold.
Life's essence, a work of art,
In every shadow, lies the heart.

Murmurs of Forgotten Dreams

In twilight whispers, shadows loom,
Old echoes linger, filled with gloom.
Lost wishes dance on the breeze,
Fleeting hopes that fail to seize.

Time wraps softly around their flight,
In silent corners, faded light.
They flutter gently, a silken thread,
Of all the things left unsaid.

Every sigh tells a tale untold,
Of vibrant colors now turned cold.
In quiet chambers of the heart,
The dreams we cherish drift apart.

Yet in the stillness, a spark may glow,
A glimmer of what we used to know.
In the vaults of memory, we find our stream,
Murmurs alive, birthed from a dream.

Tales of the Unseen

Beneath the surface, stories lie,
In shadows cast by the evening sky.
Whispers float on the gentle air,
Unraveled secrets, unaware.

Footsteps echo in the night,
Faint glimmers of lost light.
Figures dance in the periphery,
Tales unfold, yet never free.

The heartbeats of those unseen,
Tell of battles fought, serene.
Winds carry echoes of their plight,
In the fabric of the night.

History cloaked in silence vast,
Bridges built and shadows cast.
In the dusk, they softly speak,
Of dreams and truths that stay unique.

Resonance of Lost Journeys

Footprints fade on a winding road,
Chasing sunsets, bearing a load.
Every turn, a choice once made,
In the heart, memories invade.

The path may curve and lead astray,
Yet echoes of the past will stay.
Whispers of laughter, tones of cries,
Resonance that never dies.

With every step, a story unfolds,
Adventures ventured, yet untold.
Roots of yesterday intertwine,
In the soul's soft design.

Time may stretch and wane like night,
But the journeys fuel our inner light.
In restless dreams, we'll always roam,
Resonance leads us back home.

The Secret Life of Mist

In morning's hush, the mist does creep,
Veiling secrets, depths so deep.
A gentle shroud on the sleeping earth,
Whispers of magic, stories of birth.

It dances lightly, kiss of the dawn,
Caressing petals, then it's gone.
Veils adorned with dew's embrace,
Masking the world in a silken lace.

Through branches swaying, a dreamlike hue,
The mist reveals what the sun renews.
In fleeting moments, it threads the skies,
Painting visions with cloudy sighs.

To the wandering heart, it gives a song,
In shadows where the echoes belong.
The secret life whispers, sublime,
Where the mist softly dances with time.

Milton Keynes UK
Ingram Content Group UK Ltd.
UKHW022006131124
451149UK00013B/1024

9 789916 888612